LIGHT
FRUIT DESSERTS

CONTENTS

FRUIT COMPOTES—THREE WAYS

The Mediterranean

The Middle East

Northern & Eastern Europe

$\mathcal{L}$IGHT FRUIT DESSERTS FROM AROUND THE WORLD

Whether they are prepared with ingredients from local orchards or with exotic produce from far-off lands, fruit desserts are always popular with young and old alike.

ASIA & THE FAR EAST

This region offers an exceptionally rich variety of fruits—such as mangos, papayas, and litchis—which are prepared in traditional ways and relished as delicacies. These wonderfully colorful light desserts are easy to create with local produce and other ingredients. Chinese toffee apples and coconut rice with mango and papaya are among the delicious offerings that you can easily make at home.

Mangos, kiwis, guavas, and other fresh produce offer daily enticements at Caribbean markets. The balmy tropical climate allows exotic fruits to ripen all year round. We've

NORTH AMERICA & AUSTRALASIA

Cobblers, flambés, and fruit salads are just a few of the alluring desserts we've collected from the U.S. and Canada, and Australia and New Zealand. Nuts, cinnamon, and honey are popular added ingredients.

THE MEDITERRANEAN

NORTHERN & EASTERN EUROPE

Apples, cherries, pears, and several varieties of berries are harvested in the many orchards and farms of this part of the world. These fruits are often combined with pastry or cream in irresistible desserts like English trifle and berry parfait.

THE MIDDLE EAST

Sweet and juicy fruits are special delicacies in the Middle East, since the heat and aridity of this region often limits their availability. Israel's excellent irrigation system makes it an exception to the rule—this country's bounty of fruit is temptingly diverse. Popular ingredients throughout the area include figs, dates, apricots, and grapes.

imported an array of recipes for exquisite yet simple treats—like fruit combinations flavored with coconut milk, rum, or fruit juice—that you'll love to make and eat.

Fruit refreshments are much loved throughout the Mediterranean. Many imaginative dessert recipes have originated here, such as the famous stuffed peaches from Piedmont or Melon Basket Provençal.

ℳANGO AND COCONUT MOUSSE

Sweet, slightly spicy mango and creamy coconut are the featured flavors of this velvety mousse. It's the perfect dessert for entertaining—make it ahead of time, then simply let it chill.

INGREDIENTS
(Serves 4)

- 1 package unflavored gelatin
- ¾ cup unsweetened coconut milk
- 2 eggs, separated
- 3 tablespoons dark rum
- 2 tablespoons lime juice
- ½ teaspoon vanilla extract
- 3 tablespoons sugar
- pinch of salt
- 2 ripe mangos
- ½ cup heavy cream
- pinch of cream of tartar
- cocoa powder and mint leaves for garnish

INGREDIENT TIP

Select plump, heavy mangos that are firm yet tender when pressed (like an avocado). Avoid fruit with soft spots or flabby, wrinkled skin.

1 Place ¼ cup of cold water in a small saucepan. Sprinkle the gelatin on top; let soften for 2 minutes. Stir over low heat until mixture is clear. Stir in the coconut milk.

2 In a large bowl, mix the egg yolks, rum, lime juice, vanilla, 1 tablespoon sugar, and the salt. Set over a saucepan containing 1 inch of hot water. Over low heat, whisk until thickened, 5–7 minutes. Mix in the gelatin mixture and cool for 20 minutes.

3 Peel the mangos. Cut the flesh of one mango from the pit, score into cubes, and cut from the skin. Puree in a food processor. Pit and slice the second mango.

4 In a medium bowl, beat the cream until stiff. Fold into the mango puree. Over a saucepan of simmering water, beat the egg whites with 2 tablespoons sugar, 1 teaspoon water, and the cream of tartar until stiff, about 4 minutes. Fold into the mango mixture. Pour into a bowl, cover, and refrigerate for 3 hours or until set.

5 Sprinkle 4 plates with cocoa. Arrange scoopfuls of mousse and several mango slices on each. Garnish with mint leaves.

Step 2

Step 3

Step 4

Preparation: 45 minutes
Chilling: 3 hours
Per serving: 374 cal; 7 g pro; 24 g fat; 30 g carb.

TYPICALLY JAMAICAN

World-famous Jamaican rum is distilled from the sugarcane plant, which thrives in the hot, sunny climate of the Caribbean. The rums of other West Indian islands, as well as those from elsewhere, each have their own distinctive character.

COOKING TIP

It's quite easy to make coconut milk yourself. Simmer 1 cup hot water and 1 cup dried unsweetened coconut until frothy, about 20 minutes. Then strain the liquid through cheese cloth.

SERVING TIPS

Serve some cold coconut milk as a beverage. Add an exotic touch by decorating the table with tropical fruits, such as mangos and coconuts.

SERVING TIP This beautiful dessert is perfect for a large gathering—simply double or triple the recipe as needed, then arrange the sliced fruits on a large platter with the rum sauce on the side.

TROPICAL FRUIT SALAD WITH RUM SAUCE

BARBADOS

An ever-popular vacation spot, the island of Barbados gives us this colorful Caribbean fruit salad laced with a sultry rum sauce. It's refreshing and delicious!

INGREDIENTS
(Serves 4)

- 1 coconut
- 1 mango
- 1 orange
- 2 figs
- 1 guava, kiwi, or star fruit
- ½ cup heavy cream
- 1 tablespoon sugar
- 2–3 tablespoons white rum

INGREDIENT TIPS

- Only ripe, juicy guavas will give you the sweet taste you want. Look for fruit that has a strong aroma and is soft to the touch.
- Use chilled fruits for added refreshing flavor. For convenience, the fruit plates can be assembled ahead and refrigerated until serving.

1 Open the coconut shell as described in the glossary. Wrap half of the coconut in plastic wrap for later use. Pare a quarter of the remaining coconut into thin strips and set aside. Finely grate the rest, place in a bowl, and add ½ cup hot water. Let stand for 15 minutes, stirring frequently.

2 Peel the mango and cut the flesh from the pit in thin slices. Peel the orange, remove the white membrane, and cut out the sections. Rinse the figs, pat dry, and cut into quarters. Peel the guava, cut in half, remove the seeds, and cut into thin strips.

3 Line a colander with a dish towel. Put in the softened, grated coconut, then squeeze the coconut milk into a bowl. Discard the grated coconut. In a medium bowl, whip the cream and sugar until stiff. Stir in ½ cup of the coconut milk and the rum.

4 Distribute equal amounts of the fruits onto 4 large chilled plates. Scatter the coconut strips on top. Serve the rum sauce on the side.

Step 1

Step 1

Step 3

Preparation: 1 hour

Per serving: 359 cal; 3 g pro; 26 g fat; 29 g carb.

TYPICALLY BARBADOS

Sugarcane and exotic fruits like the ones featured in this dish are in abundance on the lush tropical island of Barbados. They go hand in hand as rum, distilled from sugarcane, easily finds its way into fruity drinks and desserts.

CARIBBEAN ORANGE BASKETS

THE BAHAMAS

This colorful and refreshing mixture of sweet and tangy fruits is presented in orange cups, which make naturally beautiful compote dishes that are just the right size for a single serving.

INGREDIENTS
(Serves 4)

- 2 large navel oranges
- 1 pink grapefruit
- 1 tangerine or clementine
- 2 small kiwis
- ½ cup fresh red currants, raspberries, or blueberries
- 1 lime
- 1 tablespoon sugar
- ¼ cup coconut liqueur
- 1 small banana

INGREDIENT TIP

You can use white rum mixed with coconut milk or a tropical fruit juice, such as pineapple juice, instead of coconut liqueur.

1 Cut the navel oranges in half. Cut out the sections over a large bowl along the membrane, catching the juice. Remove the orange membranes from the rind with a paring knife or grapefruit spoon to make a hollow cup from the orange half.

Step 1

2 Peel the grapefruit and catch the juice in the bowl with the oranges while cutting out sections from the membrane. Halve the sections and add to the orange sections. Peel and section the tangerine and add to the other fruit. Peel and dice the kiwis and add to the fruit. Remove the stems from the currants and add the currants to the fruit.

Step 2

3 Grate the lime with a fine grater to remove 1 teaspoon of the peel, then squeeze the juice into a medium bowl. Add the grated peel, sugar, and liqueur. Mix well.

4 Peel the banana, cut into slices, and add to the lime mixture, tossing to coat with the liquid. Add to the fruit and mix gently. Spoon into the orange peel cups.

Step 4

Preparation: 25 minutes
Per serving: 197 cal; 2 g pro; 0 g fat; 1 g carb.

TYPICALLY CARIBBEAN

The year-round temperate climate of the Caribbean is perfect for producing the fruit from which islanders prepare salads like the one shown here. The Spaniards introduced oranges, limes, and bananas to the region.

COOKING TIPS

• Cut off a thin slice from the bottom of the orange rinds so that they are more stable when filled with the fruit salad.

• The lime peel can be rubbed off with a sugar cube, which can then be mixed in with the other ingredients.

SERVING TIPS

Chunks of fresh coconut, placed on the table in a dish of ice-cold water make a delicious addition. Or serve the orange baskets with whipped cream flavored with grated coconut.

TEQUILA-SPLASHED PINEAPPLE AND BANANA

MEXICO

Ripe bananas and juicy pineapple—coated in a buttery glaze of brown sugar and tequila and sprinkled with curls of chocolate —is a delicious combination of sweet and fruity.

INGREDIENTS
(Serves 4)

- 1 small pineapple
- 4 small firm, ripe bananas
- 1½ ounces milk chocolate
- 4 tablespoons butter
- 3 tablespoons brown sugar
- ¼ cup tequila or white rum

INGREDIENT TIP

Despite their prickly skin, pineapples are very sensitive: They bruise easily. Also, they should be stored at room temperature until cut.

1 Remove the crown from the pineapple. Carefully pare away the skin, cutting out all the hard dark eyes with a paring knife. Quarter, core, and cube the pineapple.

2 Peel the bananas and cut in half length-wise. Shave the chocolate into small curls with a vegetable peeler and set aside.

3 Melt 2 tablespoons butter in a large saucepan over medium-high heat. Stir in the brown sugar. When the sugar is melted, add the pineapple and cook, stirring, for 5 minutes. Remove to a plate.

4 Pour the tequila into the drippings in the saucepan. Sauté for 1 minute, until the liquid evaporates. Melt the remaining 2 tablespoons butter until foamy. Place the bananas cut-side up in the pan; cook for 2 minutes. Carefully turn over with a spatula and add the pineapple. Heat through for 2 minutes.

5 Place 2 banana halves on each of 4 plates, top with the hot pineapple and sprinkle with the chocolate. Serve warm.

Step 1

Step 2

Step 3

Preparation: 20 minutes
Cooking: 12 minutes
Per serving: 414 cal; 3 g pro; 16 g fat; 62 g carb.

TYPICALLY MEXICAN

Tequila, the national drink of Mexico, is distilled from the sap of a variety of agave plant. Besides imbibing it, Mexicans use the liquor as an ingredient in a number of delectable desserts.

COOKING TIPS

• Be careful not to overheat the butter, and to melt but not caramelize the brown sugar and pineapple-juice syrup.

• The pineapple can be peeled and cubed a day beforehand; cover it well and refrigerate.

SERVING TIPS

Place a bowl of pineapples, lemons, and bananas on the table to add a colorful touch. The dessert is extra-delicious served with vanilla or coffee ice cream.

PEACH-BLUEBERRY COBBLER

USA

Here, a crispy golden crust hides juicy peaches and sweet blueberries. Serve these individual cakes straight from the oven, topped with a scoop of vanilla ice cream.

INGREDIENTS

(Serves 4)

- 3 ripe peaches
- 1 pint blueberries
- 6 tablespoons soft butter
- ⅓ cup sugar
- 1 large egg
- ¾ cup flour
- 1 teaspoon baking powder
- ¼ teaspoon cinnamon
- ⅓ cup milk

IN ADDITION

- butter for the crocks
- 4 scoops of vanilla ice cream

INGREDIENT TIPS

- If you plan to use frozen berries, use the same amount and don't thaw them first.
- In the autumn, tart apples are an excellent substitute for peaches.

1 Preheat the oven to 375°F. Generously grease four 12-ounce ovenproof crocks or custard cups with butter.

2 Wash and quarter the peaches lengthwise and remove the pits. Cut these quarters into thin slices.

Step 2

3 Carefully rinse the berries with water in a colander. Pat dry and stem. Combine the peaches and berries and distribute them among the prepared crocks.

4 In a bowl, cream the butter and sugar until fluffy. Beat in the egg until thoroughly incorporated.

Step 4

5 Mix the flour, baking powder, and cinnamon together. Alternately stir into the butter mixture with the milk. Spoon the batter over the fruit.

6 Put the crocks in the oven and bake for about 35 minutes or until golden brown. Place one scoop of vanilla ice cream on top of each and serve.

Step 5

Preparation: 25 minutes

Baking: 35 minutes

Per serving: 534 cal; 8 g pro; 29 g fat; 65 g carb.

TYPICALLY TEXAN

In sunny Texas, it isn't hard to find juicy gold and yellow peaches as well as sweet blueberries. The area around the Colorado River is an especially fertile region for fruit and vegetable farming.

COOKING TIP

For a more delicate variation of this cobbler, peel the peaches before use by scoring an X in their skins and blanching them quickly in boiling water or pouring boiling water over them and letting them sit a minute. Rinse in cold water and carefully strip the skin off with a sharp knife.

SERVING TIP

Skip the ice cream and serve a blueberry milkshake alongside—kids love it. Simply put ⅔ cup blueberries, 2 cups milk, and 4 ice cubes into a blender; whip until smooth. Pour the shakes into glasses. Garnish with fresh mint leaves.

ℬOURBON-BANANA FLAMBÉ

USA

The vibrant flavors of New Orleans are all here in this flaming dessert—an irresistible pairing of bourbon and brown sugar–glazed bananas and homemade vanilla ice cream.

INGREDIENTS

(Serves 4)

FOR THE ICE CREAM
- 1 vanilla bean
- 1½ cups heavy cream
- ¼ cup sugar
- pinch of salt

FOR THE BANANAS
- 4 small bananas
- 4 tablespoons butter
- 3 tablespoons brown sugar
- ¼ teaspoon cinnamon
- ¼ cup banana or coffee liqueur
- ¼ cup bourbon

INGREDIENT TIP

You can use 1 teaspoon vanilla extract in place of the vanilla bean. Or use prepared ice cream.

1 Split the vanilla bean lengthwise with a sharp knife and scrape the seeds into a small saucepan. Add the bean, heavy cream, sugar, and salt, and stir. Steep over low heat for 15 minutes, but do not boil. Let cool.

2 Remove the vanilla bean from the mixture and pour the cream into an ice-cream maker. Freeze according to the manufacturer's instructions.

3 Peel and cut the bananas in half lengthwise. Heat the butter, brown sugar, and cinnamon in a large skillet over medium heat until everything has melted.

4 Place the banana halves in the pan and warm for 3 minutes, shifting the pan gently every so often. Scoop the vanilla ice cream onto 4 dessert dishes.

5 Remove the skillet from the heat. Pour the banana liqueur and bourbon over the bananas and light with a long match. Let the flames die out. Place the bananas and sauce over the vanilla ice cream and serve immediately.

Step 1

Step 3

Step 5

Preparation: 30 minutes
Freezing: 5 hours
Per serving: 619 cal; 3 g pro; 45 g fat; 49 g carb.

TYPICALLY LOUISIANA

New Orleans' jazz is as prized in this city as the bourbon for which one of its most famous streets is named. The spirit of choice in the southern states, this flavorful liquor is used frequently in cakes and dessert dishes.

COOKING TIPS

• The vanilla ice cream can be prepared several days in advance and kept frozen.

• When lighting the bananas, use a long match and hold the pan at a safe distance.

SERVING TIP

Light the bananas at the table as a treat for your guests. Dim the lights for the best effect.

SERVING TIPS Offer this pretty fruit dish with its yogurt cream as a light ending to a hearty meal. Or, include it as part of a brunch menu. Garnish the individual bowls with sprigs of fresh mint.

ℐWEET MAPLE FRUIT DELIGHT

Maple syrup—the ambrosial sweetener from Canada and the northern United States—adds its unique sugary flavor to this tossed blend of colorful fresh fruits.

INGREDIENTS
(Serves 4)

- 1 pint raspberries
- 1 pint blackberries
- 1 pint red currants
- 4 small Italian plums or 8 damsons
- 1 small peach
- ¼ cup pure maple syrup
- 3 tablespoons lemon juice
- 1 tart apple

IN ADDITION

- ½ cup heavy cream
- ½ cup plain yogurt
- 2 tablespoons pure maple syrup
- 2 tablespoons chopped walnuts

INGREDIENT TIP

If you can't find red currants, substitute an equal amount of raspberries, blackberries, blueberries, or strawberries.

1 Wash the raspberries, blackberries, and red currants gently and sort. Strip off the stems of the currants with a fork. Wash the plums and peach, then pit and cut them into thin slices.

Step 1

2 In a small bowl, whisk the maple syrup with 2 tablespoons lemon juice until smooth. Quarter, peel, and core the apple. Thinly slice the quarters and sprinkle with the remaining 1 tablespoon lemon juice to prevent browning.

3 Carefully mix all of the fruit with the maple-lemon mixture in a bowl, cover, and refrigerate for at least 1 hour (and up to 4 hours).

Step 2

4 Just before serving, beat the heavy cream until it is not quite stiff. Fold in the yogurt and maple syrup.

5 Divide the fruit among glass dessert dishes and put some of the yogurt cream on top of each. Sprinkle the chopped walnuts on top.

Step 3

Preparation: 30 minutes
Chilling: 1 hour
Per serving: 349 cal; 5 g pro; 15 g fat; 55 g carb.

TYPICALLY CANADIAN
The sugar maple trees of Canada provide the raw material for its ever-popular syrup. The sap drips slowly out of the tapped trunks and then undergoes a heating process that thickens it to yield the amber syrup.

𝓛USCIOUS KIWI-STRAWBERRY SALAD

NEW ZEALAND

INGREDIENTS
(Serves 4)

- 1 pint large strawberries
- 4 kiwis
- 2 tablespoons lemon juice
- 2 tablespoons honey
- 2 tablespoons orange liqueur or orange juice
- pinch of cinnamon
- 2 tablespoons sliced almonds

INGREDIENT TIP

Kiwis should give a little to the touch, but not be too soft. To ripen hard kiwis, put them into a brown paper bag with a piece of ripe fruit, which accelerates the ripening process.

Fresh strawberries and kiwis form a delicious composition in red and green, accompanied by a tangy orange syrup. Golden brown roasted almonds provide the crunch.

1 Rinse the strawberries and pat dry with a paper towel. Cut or pull out the leaves as well as the hull of the strawberries with a paring knife. Peel kiwis with the knife.

2 Cut the strawberries and kiwis into ¼-inch-thick slices. Arrange the fruit in overlapping layers on a serving dish.

3 In a small bowl, mix the lemon juice, honey, liqueur, and cinnamon until blended to make the orange dressing. Drizzle the fruit with the dressing. Cover the salad and refrigerate for 1 hour to let the flavors develop.

4 Toast the almonds in a dry skillet over medium heat until golden brown. Set aside. Before serving, sprinkle the almonds over the fruit.

Step 1

Step 2

Step 3

Preparation: 25 minutes
Chilling: 1 hour
Per serving: 142 cal; 2 g pro;
2 g fat; 29 g carb.

TYPICALLY NEW ZEALAND

Once known as the Chinese gooseberry, kiwi fruit was cleverly named by New Zealanders after their own native bird, the kiwi (left). Their promotional efforts have sent this small, unpretentious-looking fruit on a triumphant march around the world. New Zealand is now considered the popular fruit's homeland.

COOKING TIP

Use a nonstick skillet and medium to medium-low heat to toast the almonds. Watch them carefully and stir frequently to keep them from browning too much or too quickly.

SERVING TIP

For an extra-special treat, serve this salad with waffle cones and a dollop of some softly whipped heavy cream.

*M*ELON—THREE WAYS

Melons make attractive, delicious serving bowls for various fruit fillings. Here are three decorative variations.

WATERMELON WITH HONEY CREAM

Preparation: 20 minutes   Draining: 1 hour

TURKEY

(SERVES 4)
- ½ watermelon
- 1-inch piece fresh ginger
- 1 tablespoon lemon juice
- 2 tablespoons plus
  1 teaspoon honey
- 2 cups plain yogurt
- 1 tablespoon chopped
  fresh mint

1 Seed the watermelon and scoop out the flesh in balls. Scrape out the remaining pulp. Cut a slice off the bottom of the melon so that it stands upright.

2 Peel and mince the ginger. In a large bowl, mix the ginger with the lemon juice and 1 teaspoon honey. Add the melon balls and mix gently. Cover and refrigerate until serving time.

3 Stir the yogurt well. Place in a cheesecloth-lined sieve suspended over a bowl; let drain for 1 hour. Stir in the remaining 2 tablespoons honey and the mint.

4 Place three quarters of the melon balls in the melon rind, spoon the honey cream over them, and then top with the remaining melon balls. Serve immediately.

MELON BASKET

Preparation: 45 minutes

FRANCE

(SERVES 4)
- 2 small cantaloupes
- 1 cup *each* seedless red
  and green grapes
- 1 kiwi
- 2 small figs
- ½ cup white wine
- 1 tablespoon lemon juice
- 1 tablespoon orange juice
- 1 tablespoon sugar
- 1 tablespoon slivered
  almonds

1 Cut the melon in half, making a scalloped edge if desired. Remove the seeds and scoop out the flesh in balls. Cut a slice from the bottom of the melons so they stand upright.

CHILLED MELON SOUP

Preparation: 30 minutes   Chilling: 2 hours

SPAIN

(SERVES 4)
- **2 honeydew melons**
- **2 teaspoons sugar**
- **juice from 1 lemon**
- **2 oranges**
- **1 tablespoon sliced almonds**
- **mint leaves**

1 Cut the melons in half, remove the seeds, and scoop out the flesh with a spoon. Cut off a slice from the bottom of the rinds so that the melons stand upright. Cut the melon flesh into large pieces.

2 Puree the melon in a food processor with the sugar and lemon juice. Cover and refrigerate for 2 hours.

3 Peel one orange and remove the sections from the membrane. Cut the remaining orange in half and then into slices.

4 Lightly toast the almonds in a dry skillet over medium heat, stirring, for 1–2 minutes, until golden. Stir the chilled soup and pour it into the melon rinds. Arrange the orange sections on top. Garnish with the almonds, mint leaves, and orange slices.

PROVENÇAL

Chilling: 1 hour

2 Cut the grapes in half. Peel the kiwi. Wash the figs and remove the stem. Cut the kiwi and figs into 1-inch cubes.

3 In a large bowl, mix the wine, lemon and orange juices, and the sugar. Carefully mix in the fruit; cover and refrigerate for 1 hour.

4 Toast the almonds in a dry skillet over medium heat, stirring, for 1–2 minutes until golden. Place the fruit in the melon rinds and sprinkle with the almonds. Serve immediately.

CREAMY COCONUT RICE WITH FRUIT

THAILAND

INGREDIENTS
(Serves 4)

- ¾ cup Asian short-grain sticky rice
- 1 cup unsweetened coconut milk
- ⅓ cup sugar
- 1 small papaya
- 1 small mango
- ½ teaspoon rose water or grated lime peel
- ¼ cup pineapple or orange juice
- 1 teaspoon slivered lime peel
- pecan halves for garnish

INGREDIENT TIP

If you can't find sticky rice, use 1 cup regular short- or long-grain white rice and 2¼ cups milk instead of the water in Step 1. Add a pinch of salt and cook, covered, for 25 minutes. Sweeten with 5 tablespoons of the coconut syrup; set aside for 1 hour.

This delightful dessert rounds out a light Southeast Asian meal perfectly. Your family and guests will love the exotic flavor combination of coconut rice with mango and papaya.

1 Rinse the rice in cold water and place in a small saucepan. Add 1¼ cups water and bring to a boil. Cover and cook for 18 minutes over low heat.

2 In a medium bowl, stir the coconut milk with the sugar until the sugar dissolves. Mix ¼ cup of this coconut syrup into the cooked rice, cover, and set aside in a cool place for 1 hour.

3 Halve the papaya and remove the seeds with a spoon. Peel the halves with a sharp knife and cut the flesh into thin slices. Peel the mango with the knife and slice the flesh from the pit in thin slices.

4 In a large bowl, mix the rose water with the pineapple juice. Add the fruit slices and gently mix to coat with the liquid. Arrange the fruit and rice on dessert plates and top with the remaining coconut syrup. Garnish with the lime peel and pecans.

Step 3

Step 4

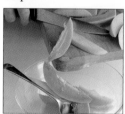

Step 4

Preparation: 35 minutes
Cooling: 1 hour
Per serving: 359 cal; 4 g pro;
12 g fat; 60 g carb.

TYPICALLY THAI

Rice, one of the most important staples in the Thai kitchen, is very adaptable and even goes well with fruit. Tropical Thailand enjoys an abundant variety of fruits, including mangos and papayas. Several different types of mangos are cultivated there.

COOKING TIP

Toasting the pecans will bring out their flavor and provide a crunchy contrast to the rice and fruit. Spread out the nuts on a baking sheet and bake in a 375°F oven for 5-8 minutes, until aromatic.

SERVING TIP

For an attractive presentation, place the rice in medium-size bowls and layer the fruit next to it. Then decorate the dessert with the leaves of exotic fruits.

CHINESE TOFFEE APPLES

CHINA

These small tasty apples are very popular in Northern China. A crunchy delicacy, they're wrapped in batter, fried until crispy, and covered with golden caramel.

INGREDIENTS

(Serves 4)

FOR THE DOUGH

- 2 large eggs
- 1¼ cups all-purpose flour
- 1 cup white wine
- 1 tablespoon sugar
- pinch of salt

FOR THE APPLES

- 8 very small, firm apples
- vegetable oil for frying
- ½ cup sugar
- 4 tablespoons butter, cubed
- ¼ cup heavy cream
- 2 tablespoons sesame seeds, lightly toasted

INGREDIENT TIP

Use a neutral oil for frying, one that does not have a strong flavor. Safflower, sunflower, and peanut oils are all good choices.

1 Separate the eggs. Place yolks in a bowl and add the flour, wine, sugar, and salt. Stir until smooth. Refrigerate for 30 minutes.

2 Peel and core the apples. In a large deep saucepan, heat the oil to 350°F or until bubbles surround a wooden spoon handle.

3 In a medium bowl, beat the egg whites until stiff and gently fold into the batter. Turn the apples in the batter until covered.

4 Fry the apples in the oil for about 3 minutes, until golden. Remove with a slotted spoon and drain on paper towels.

5 In a saucepan, bring the ½ cup sugar and 2 tablespoons water to a boil, stirring, over high heat. Stop stirring and let the sugar cook for 3 minutes, until caramelized, swirling the pan occasionally. Turn off the heat; carefully stir in the butter until smooth (caramel may splatter). Stir in the heavy cream.

6 Place 2 apples on each of 4 dessert plates. Pour the caramel around the sides and sprinkle with sesame seeds.

Step 2

Step 2

Step 3

Preparation: 15 minutes
Chilling: 30 minutes
Cooking: 10 minutes
Per serving: 702 cal; 9 g pro; 32 g fat; 90 g carb.

TYPICALLY BEIJING

Small, flowering crab apples have been favorites in Beijing for centuries, since they were planted on the grounds of the Imperial Palace. Today, apples are still popular in the region, where they are often served after a meal, either simply sliced or made into crispy caramel-coated fritters.

COOKING TIPS

• If no small apples are available, large ones can be quartered or cut into thick wedges and fried.

• When preparing the caramel, use only a wooden spoon; a plastic spoon will melt at the high temperatures you must use to brown the sugar.

SERVING TIP

Plain, unsweetened tea usually accompanies a Chinese meal from the appetizer to dessert. And it tastes particularly nice with these toffee apples.

27

TANGY ORANGE-AVOCADO SALAD

INGREDIENTS
(Serves 4)

- 3 large oranges
- orange juice
- 2 tablespoons sugar
- dash of ground aniseed
- pinch of cinnamon
- 1 avocado
- 2 tablespoons lemon juice
- 6 pitted dates

INGREDIENT TIP

You can use any number of spices in place of ground anise. Try a pinch of ground allspice, ginger, nutmeg, or coriander.

After one bite, no one can resist this refreshing dessert from Israel. Made with juicy oranges and creamy avocados, this dish is also a great source of vitamins.

1 Wash the oranges in hot water and dry. Strip off the peel from one of the oranges with a vegetable peeler or pare it off using a small sharp knife. Cut the rind into thin strips. There should be about 1 tablespoon.

2 Peel the other two oranges and separate the sections from the membrane, saving the juice that drips off. Halve the peeled orange and squeeze out the remaining juice. There should be about 1 cup all together. Add some orange juice if not.

3 Combine the juice, orange peel, sugar, anise, and cinnamon in a small pot over medium-high heat; boil, stirring occasionally, for 15 minutes, until reduced slightly.

4 Halve the avocados and remove the pit. Peel off the skin and cut crosswise into slices. Sprinkle the avocado slices with the lemon juice to keep them from browning.

5 Arrange the prepared orange sections and avocado slices on 4 plates and pour the orange syrup over them. Cut the dates into strips and sprinkle over the salad.

Step 2

Step 3

Step 4

Preparation: 30 minutes
Cooking: 15 minutes
Per serving: 219 cal; 2 g pro; 8 g fat; 39 g carb.

TYPICALLY ISRAELI

According to Jewish dietary laws, fruit can be eaten after both meat and dairy meals, which is why fruit desserts are especially popular among families who keep kosher households. Avocados, dates, and oranges are all grown in Israel.

COOKING TIPS

• You can tell whether or not an avocado is ripe if it gives slightly when pressed with your thumb.

• Sliced avocados discolor quite rapidly. Always sprinkle them with a little lemon juice to prevent this from happening.

SERVING TIP

Crispy almond cookies make a fine accompaniment to this juicy fruit salad.

29

SERVING TIP For a creative, eye-catching presentation, serve the ice in scooped-out orange halves and garnish with orange sections. You will need two extra oranges to do this.

ORANGE ICE DREAM

This cooling, low-fat ice hails from Iran. It takes only minutes to make and is an ideal do-ahead dessert—simply let it freeze until you're ready for a crowning finale to any meal.

INGREDIENTS
(Serves 4)

- 3 large navel oranges
- ⅓ cup sugar
- 1 tablespoon honey
- 2 tablespoons lemon juice
- 4 dried or fresh dates
- orange leaves (optional)
- 2 tablespoons chopped pistachio nuts

INGREDIENT TIPS

- Use fresh dates if you can find them—they're a tasty alternative to dried.
- Middle Eastern desserts are often given extra flavor with a few drops of rose water—a variation worth trying.

1 Grate 1 tablespoon peel from 1 orange and place in a small saucepan. Add the juice from all the oranges, the sugar, and honey. Heat, stirring constantly, over low heat until the sugar and honey dissolve.

2 Remove the saucepan from the heat and stir in the lemon juice. Pour into an 8-inch square pan, place in a roasting pan with enough ice and water to come halfway up the sides of the square pan, and let the orange mixture stand until cool.

3 Cover the orange mixture with foil and freeze for 4 hours, until firm, stirring the mixture several times with a whisk during freezing to break up the slush and to help the ice freeze evenly.

4 While the ice freezes, pit and slice the dates with a sharp knife. To serve, stir the ice and scoop it into chilled dessert dishes. Garnish with the dates and orange leaves and sprinkle with the pistachios.

Step 1

Step 1

Step 4

Preparation: 30 minutes
Freezing: 4 hours
Per serving: 185 cal; 2 g pro;
2 g fat; 42 g carb.

TYPICALLY IRANIAN
Oranges originated in Southeast Asia and are now grown in warm-climate areas all over the world. In the Middle East, these fruits are widely cultivated and play an important part in the cuisine of the region.

ℛ ASPBERRY CREAM PARFAITS

INGREDIENTS
(Serves 4)

- 2 tablespoons rolled oats
- 1¼ cups heavy cream
- 3 tablespoons honey
- 1 tablespoon whiskey
- 1½ pints raspberries or strawberries

IN ADDITION

- 2 tablespoons butter
- 4 tablespoons rolled oats

INGREDIENT TIP

Although Scotch whiskey (sometimes known just as Scotch), is the most traditional flavoring for this creamy parfait, if you prefer, you can substitute an equal amount of orange juice.

In this Scottish dessert, delicious raspberries, honeyed whipped cream, and whiskey make a unique composition that you'll want to indulge in again and again.

1 Roast 2 tablespoons rolled oats in a dry pan over medium heat for about 5 minutes. Remove from the pan and let cool.

2 Beat the heavy cream with a mixer until stiff peaks form. Blend in the honey and whiskey little by little. Fold in the cooled roasted oats.

3 Wash the raspberries carefully, allow them to drip dry, then sort and remove any remaining stem parts.

4 Place the raspberries and cream mixture in alternating layers into 4 tall parfait glasses, starting with raspberries and finishing with cream. Garnish the top layer with raspberries and refrigerate for 2 hours.

5 Heat the butter in a small pan until it foams. Add the 4 tablespoons rolled oats and cook, stirring, for 1–2 minutes, or until golden brown. Remove from the heat and let cool. Sprinkle the toasted rolled oats over the dessert just before serving.

Step 1

Step 2

Step 4

Preparation: 30 minutes
Chilling: 2 hours
Per serving: 438 cal; 4 g pro; 34 g fat; 31 g carb.

TYPICALLY SCOTTISH

Pristine waters, barley, and peat are the basic requirements for the production of the Scottish elixir of life: genuine malt whiskey. It matures in charred barrels for a minimum of three years, which lends it mellowness. Its characteristic pale yellow to brown color comes from burnt sugar.

COOKING TIP

For a pretty, pink-hued variation of this Scottish cream, make a puree with half the raspberries and carefully fold it into the whiskey cream. Then layer some of the whole berries and the cream in tall glasses and garnish with the remaining berries.

SERVING TIP

You can garnish the cream with whole mint leaves, pistachios, or roasted almond slivers.

TRADITIONAL ENGLISH TRIFLE

ENGLAND

Trifle, a much-loved English dessert, is a sublime combination of cake, fresh fruits, and custard. You can be sure there'll be no leftovers if you serve it at parties or other celebrations.

INGREDIENTS
(Serves 8–10)

- 6 peaches
- 1 quart strawberries
- ¼ cup sugar
- 1 prepared sponge cake (about 14 ounces)
- ¾ cup sweet sherry or peach nectar
- 1 package (2¾ ounces) instant vanilla pudding mix
- 2 cups milk
- 1 cup heavy cream

INGREDIENT TIPS

To save work and time, use:
- Prepared fruit salad from the salad bar, found in many large supermarkets.
- Refrigerated ready-to-eat pudding or french vanilla yogurt instead of pudding.
- No-cook instant pudding mix instead of one that requires cooking.

1 In a large saucepan of boiling water, blanch the peaches for 1 minute and rinse with cold water. Peel, pit, and cut into cubes, then place in a large bowl.

2 Rinse the strawberries and reserve 3 with their hulls intact. Hull the remainder, cut in half lengthwise, and add to the peaches. Add 2 tablespoons sugar and mix gently.

3 Cut the sponge cake into 1½-inch cubes, place in a glass dessert bowl, and add the sherry. Toss the cake cubes gently to evenly moisten. Spoon the fruit on top.

4 Prepare the pudding with the milk according to the instructions on the package. While it is hot, pour it over the fruit. Set aside to cool. Cover and refrigerate.

5 Before serving, whip the cream with the remaining 2 tablespoons sugar until nearly stiff. Spread almost all the cream over the pudding. Whip the remainder until stiff, place in a pastry bag fitted with a rosette tip, and pipe rosettes on top. Cut the reserved strawberries in half lengthwise and place a half on each rosette. Serve from the bowl.

Step 1

Step 3

Step 4

Preparation: 40 minutes
Cooling: 30 minutes
Per serving: 395 cal; 6 g pro; 13 g fat; 61 g carb.

TYPICALLY ENGLISH

The English love sweet and creamy desserts, so it's not surprising that this smooth and fruity one is a favorite. Whether homemade or purchased at one of England's specialty-food markets, trifle is a tradition throughout the country.

COOKING TIPS
• The dessert can be prepared a day in advance through Step 4. Take it out of the refrigerator 30 minutes before serving, top with the whipped cream, and garnish with the strawberries.
• A glass serving bowl is traditional and ensures that everyone can see the colorful ingredients.

SERVING TIP
A glass of slightly sweet sherry, such as an Oloroso, is the perfect accompaniment to this enchanting fruit dessert.

SERVING TIP Children love this gelatin treat when it's prepared in animal-figure or other small molds. Garnish the figures with whipped cream and fresh fruit for a fun party dessert.

$\mathscr{S}$PARKLING FRUIT GELATIN RING

DENMARK

Red fruit in bright orange gelatin with a sweet and creamy no-cook sauce is a light delight after any meal. You can select from a variety of berries to create a stunning visual effect.

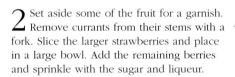

INGREDIENTS
(Serves 4)

FOR THE GELATIN
- 2 packages (3 ounces *each*) orange or peach gelatin
- 3 cups mixed berries (for example, red currants, blueberries, strawberries, raspberries, blackberries)
- 2 tablespoons sugar
- 1 tablespoon orange liqueur (optional)

FOR THE SAUCE
- ½ cup sour cream
- 2 tablespoons sugar
- 1 teaspoon lemon juice
- ¼ teaspoon vanilla extract
- ½ cup heavy cream

INGREDIENT TIP

If you use frozen berries, do not thaw them, because they will lose a lot of juice and discolor the gelatin.

1 Combine the gelatin with 2 cups boiling water in a medium bowl, and stir until dissolved. Stir in 2 cups cold water. Pour about one third of the gelatin into a 2-quart ring mold (8 or 9 inches in diameter) so that the bottom is ½-inch covered. Refrigerate just until the gelatin is set but not firm.

2 Set aside some of the fruit for a garnish. Remove currants from their stems with a fork. Slice the larger strawberries and place in a large bowl. Add the remaining berries and sprinkle with the sugar and liqueur.

3 Spoon the fruit on the set gelatin in the mold and add the remaining warm gelatin. Cover; refrigerate until set, about 3 hours.

4 In a small bowl, combine the sour cream, sugar, lemon juice, and vanilla. Mix until smooth. In another small bowl, beat the heavy cream until stiff; fold into the sour cream mixture. Unmold the gelatin ring onto a serving dish, garnish with reserved fruit, and serve with the cream sauce.

Step 2

Step 3

Step 4

Preparation: 30 minutes
Chilling: 3 hours

Per serving: 422 cal; 6 g pro; 17 g fat; 64 g carb.

TYPICALLY DANISH

Beautiful Copenhagen, with its excellent cuisine, is a favorite tourist destination and the capital of Denmark. During the holidays, Danes love extravagant buffets, or smorgasbords, which offer an enormous variety of mouthwatering dishes.

TIPSY STRAWBERRIES

UKRAINE

Fresh strawberries steeped in vodka and sugar create a sweet, aromatic sauce that is sure to tantalize your taste buds. This dessert is served with a light, creamy topping.

INGREDIENTS
(Serves 4)

- 1 pint strawberries
- 1 large orange
- ¼ cup vodka
- 3 tablespoons sugar

FOR THE TOPPING
- ⅔ cup heavy cream
- 2 tablespoons sugar
- 8 ounces cream cheese
- 5 tablespoons milk

INGREDIENT TIP
Try quark, a soft, lower-calorie cream cheese, in the topping (use less milk as you mix it). You'll find quark in cheese and specialty stores.

1 Wash the strawberries and put aside 4 especially nice ones with their leaves intact. Hull the remaining berries and halve or quarter them.

2 Wash the orange in hot water and dry. Strip off the peel from the orange with a zester or pare with a small sharp knife and then cut the rind into thin strips. Squeeze out the juice.

3 Whisk the juice with the vodka and sugar in a bowl until the sugar dissolves. Turn the strawberries in the liquid, cover, and refrigerate for 1 hour.

4 Beat the cream and sugar until stiff. Mix the cream cheese and milk in a bowl until smooth, then carefully fold in the whipped cream. Refrigerate.

5 Spoon the strawberries into 4 large dessert glasses. Dollop a generous portion of the topping over each; garnish with the whole strawberries and orange peel. Serve the leftover topping separately with the dessert.

Step 1

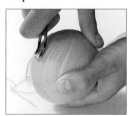
Step 2

Step 4

Preparation: 30 minutes
Chilling: 1 hour
Per serving: 484 cal; 7 g pro; 36 g fat; 29 g carb.

TYPICALLY UKRAINIAN
The Ukraine is famous for being the breadbasket of the former Soviet Union, and potatoes are one of its biggest crops. "Little water," or vodka, was originally produced from potatoes. Today Ukrainians distill it from corn, wheat, and rye.

COOKING TIP

The vodka-soaked strawberries can withstand a long marinating time—up to 1½ hours. Just be sure to keep them well covered in the refrigerator.

SERVING TIP

Break some crispy lady fingers or biscotti into large chunks and put them into the dessert glasses before adding the marinated strawberries. Or, serve whole cookies separately with the dessert.

PLUM-APRICOT COMPOTE

GERMANY

Tart, juicy plums in beautiful harmony with golden-yellow apricots make this elegant dessert as tempting to the eye as it is to the palate. It's also equally good at breakfast time.

INGREDIENTS

(Serves 4)

- 1 pound ripe damson plums or other black or red plums
- ½ pound apricots
- 1 lemon
- 1 sugar cube (optional)
- ⅓ cup plus 1 tablespoon sugar
- 2½-inch cinnamon stick
- ¼ cup plum brandy (optional)
- 1 cup heavy cream

INGREDIENT TIP

You can recognize good plums and apricots by their distinct, perfumy fragrance. Choose fruit that is ripe but not too soft so your compote has enough flavor.

1 Pit the plums and apricots, cut into thick slices, and place in a large bowl. Scrape the lemon using a sugar cube to remove the zest or grate the peel with a fine grater and add to the sliced fruits. Squeeze the juice from the lemon over the fruits and add 5 tablespoons water. Mix gently.

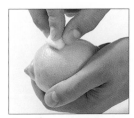

Step 1

2 Heat ⅓ cup sugar in a large saucepan over high heat and cook without stirring until a light amber caramel forms, about 3 minutes. Add the fruit mixture and simmer without stirring until the juices begin to cook out of the fruit, 3–4 minutes. Stir the fruit gently to dissolve the caramel.

Step 2

3 Add the cinnamon and bring to a boil. Cook the compote for 1 minute, cover, and simmer over low heat for 2 minutes.

4 Remove the pan from the heat and stir in 2 tablespoons of the brandy. Cool, cover, and refrigerate for at least 3 hours.

Step 3

5 Remove the cinnamon stick from the compote. Whip the cream until stiff. Beat the remaining 1 tablespoon sugar and 2 tablespoons brandy into the cream. Serve with the compote.

Preparation: 20 minutes
Cooking: 15 minutes
Chilling: 3 hours
Per serving: 369 cal; 3 g pro; 23 g fat; 42 g carb.

TYPICALLY GERMAN

Plums, used in many German desserts, are one of the most ancient cultivated fruits. The plum tree was brought from Asia to Syria and grafted by the Romans, who preserved the fruit by drying it. Apricots, too, come to us from early times; the ancient Greeks called them "golden eggs of the sun."

COOKING TIP

If you want the taste of plum brandy in the compote without the alcohol, mix the brandy into the fruit before boiling. The alcohol will evaporate, leaving a subtle aroma and flavor.

SERVING TIP

Try the compote with warm pancakes: Separate 4 eggs and beat the whites with $\frac{1}{2}$ cup sugar until stiff. Mix the yolks, $\frac{3}{4}$ cup sour cream, and $\frac{1}{2}$ cup flour until smooth. Fold the egg whites into the batter. Cook the pancakes.

✐UMMER FRUIT SALAD

GERMANY

INGREDIENTS
(Serves 4)

- 2 small lemons
- 3 tablespoons sugar
- 5 tablespoons dark or white rum or apple juice
- 1 tart apple
- 2 small kiwis
- 1 cup seedless green grapes
- 2 ripe nectarines
- ½ pint red currants or raspberries
- ½ pint strawberries
- 4 scoops vanilla ice cream

INGREDIENT TIP

To make this salad in the winter, freeze summer berries so you will have them on hand. Stem the currants and hull the strawberries. Spread out the fruit on baking sheets, freeze, then pack in freezer bags for storage.

This salad adds a beautiful dash of color to any menu. Best of all, it's easy to prepare, making it the perfect ending to a warm summer night's meal.

1 Remove the lemon peel with a fine grater and place in a large bowl. Squeeze and add the lemon juice. Add the sugar and rum.

2 Peel, halve, core, and thinly slice the apple. Add to the lemon juice mixture and toss to coat. Peel the kiwis, thinly slice, and cut the slices in half. Add to the apple.

Step 2

3 Cut the grapes in half lengthwise. Peel, pit, and thinly slice the nectarines. With a fork, strip the currants off the stems. Hull the strawberries and cut in half lengthwise. Add all of the fruits to the apple.

Step 3

4 Gently toss the fruits with the lemon-juice mixture. Place in a large glass serving bowl. Let stand for 30 minutes, stirring occasionally. Serve the fruit salad with the ice cream in glass dessert dishes.

Step 3

Preparation: 30 minutes
Standing: 30 minutes
Per serving: 340 cal; 4 g pro; 8 g fat; 57 g carb.

TYPICALLY GERMAN

Throughout Germany, there is a wide selection of fruits and berries available during the summer months in grocery stores and open markets from Munich to Hamburg.

COOKING TIP

This fruit salad can also be prepared up to 8 hours in advance. All the fruits should be thoroughly tossed in the rum and lemon mixture so they don't discolor. Keep the salad in the refrigerator until about half an hour before serving.

SERVING TIP

You might want to sprinkle the salad with chopped walnuts or hazelnuts. Or serve a dish of whole nuts on the side for people to crack at the table.

CINNAMON-APPLE FRITTERS

AUSTRIA

Juicy apples are coated with a light, crispy batter to create these yummy pastries from Austria. A sweet, creamy vanilla sauce is the finishing touch on these irresistible treats.

INGREDIENTS

(Serves 4)

- 2 tablespoons butter
- ½ cup apple juice
- 2 large eggs
- 1 cup all-purpose flour
- pinch of salt
- 3 large tart apples
- 2 tablespoons lemon juice
- ¾ cup plus 3 tablespoons sugar
- 1 teaspoon cinnamon
- vegetable oil for frying
- 1 cup sour cream
- 3 tablespoons heavy cream
- ¼ teaspoon vanilla extract

INGREDIENT TIP

Tart apples such as Cortland, Rome Beauty, and Granny Smith are choice varieties for these fritters, since the apple rings are sprinkled twice with cinnamon-sugar—before and after frying—and served with a slightly sweet sauce.

1 Melt the butter, pour into a large bowl, and stir in the apple juice. Separate the eggs and set aside the whites. Whisk the yolks, flour, and salt into the butter mixture until smooth. Cover and let stand for 1 hour.

2 Peel and core the apples. Cut crosswise into ½-inch-thick rings and place in a baking dish. Sprinkle with the lemon juice. In a small bowl, mix ¾ cup sugar and the cinnamon, and sprinkle the apple slices with half of the mixture. Let stand for 30 minutes.

3 Beat the egg whites until stiff and gently fold into the batter. In a large saucepan, heat 3 inches of oil over medium-high heat until 350°F on a deep-fry thermometer.

4 In a medium bowl, mix the sour cream, heavy cream, the remaining 3 tablespoons sugar, and the vanilla extract until smooth. Set aside.

5 Dip each apple ring in the batter to coat and carefully lower into the hot oil. Fry in batches, turning, for 2 minutes, until golden. Drain on paper towels and sprinkle on both sides with the remaining cinnamon-sugar. Serve with the sour cream sauce.

Step 1

Step 2

Step 5

Preparation: 25 minutes
Standing: 1 hour
Cooking: 20 minutes
Per serving: 498 cal; 6 g pro; 26 g fat; 63 g carb.

TYPICALLY AUSTRIAN

Apples are among the most popular fruits in Austria, where bakers often use them in pastries and fritters. Variations on this recipe occur in many European countries—it is said that fritters were brought back from the Middle East by the crusaders.

COOKING TIP

If you don't have a deep-fry thermometer or a double-duty one that also registers the temperature of syrup when making candy, you can determine if the oil is hot enough to fry the fritters by placing a wooden spoon, handle down, in the hot oil. If small bubbles appear, the oil is hot enough to begin.

SERVING TIPS

You can serve the fritters with a dish of butter pecan or vanilla ice cream instead of vanilla sauce. Break out your special coffee beans and grind them fresh for the perfect brew to complement the cinnamony fruit.

CHERRY BEIGNETS

SWITZERLAND

This enticing variety of fritter—"beignet" in French—hails from Switzerland. Bundles of sweet, soft cherries are dipped in batter and fried a crunchy, golden brown.

INGREDIENTS
(Serves 4)

- 2 large eggs
- 1¼ cups all-purpose flour
- 1 cup white wine
- 3 tablespoons sugar
- pinch of salt
- 12 ounces sweet cherries with stems
- vegetable oil for deep frying
- 1 teaspoon cinnamon

INGREDIENT TIP

Look for fresh, unbruised cherries with stems that are firmly attached.

1 Separate the eggs. In a medium bowl, whisk the yolks with the flour, wine, 1 tablespoon sugar, and salt to make a smooth batter. Cover and refrigerate for 30 minutes.

2 Rinse the cherries and drain on paper towels. Tie 3–4 cherries together by the stems with kitchen string.

3 In a large deep saucepan, heat the oil to 350°F or until small bubbles form around a wooden spoon handle.

4 In a medium bowl, beat the egg whites until stiff and gently fold into the batter. Using a fork, dip the bundles of cherries into the batter and then lower them into the hot oil. Fry for 2 minutes, until golden brown.

5 Remove the cherries with a slotted spoon and drain on paper towels. In a small bowl, mix together the remaining 2 tablespoons sugar and the cinnamon, and sprinkle the mixture over the cherries. Serve while still warm.

Step 1

Step 4

Step 5

Preparation: 15 minutes
Chilling: 30 minutes
Cooking: 8 minutes
Per serving: 393 cal; 8 g pro; 13 g fat; 53 g carb.

TYPICALLY SWISS
In many parts of Switzerland, but particularly in the picturesque Lake Lucerne area, visitors can enjoy delicious, crispy cherry beignets made with the juicy fresh-picked fruits.

PEARS BELLE HÉLÈNE

FRANCE

"Bon appetit á la française!" Pear halves, gently simmered in a delicate syrup, are transformed into a festive dessert with vanilla ice cream and warm chocolate sauce.

INGREDIENTS

(Serves 4)

- ½ vanilla bean
- ¼ cup sugar
- 2 ripe pears
- 2 ounces bittersweet chocolate
- 2 tablespoons heavy cream
- vanilla ice cream
- mint leaves for garnish

INGREDIENT TIP

Be sure to buy ripe pears that are very aromatic. Bosc and Comice pears are well suited to this dish. If you can't find good fresh pears, use canned pear halves.

1 Slit the vanilla bean lengthwise and scrape out the seeds with a knife. Put the bean, seeds, sugar, and ¼ cup water in a large saucepan. Bring to a boil, stirring.

2 Halve the pears lengthwise and remove the core carefully with a spoon or knife. Peel the pears and lay them in the vanilla syrup. Cover and simmer over low heat for 5–10 minutes, until tender. Remove the pan from the heat, allow the pears to cool in the syrup, and refrigerate for at least 2 hours.

3 Bring 1 inch of water to a boil in a large saucepan. Place an overturned custard cup in the bottom of the pan. Chop the chocolate finely, place it in a small, heat-proof bowl, and add the cream. Place the bowl in the saucepan, resting on top of the cup, so that the bottom of the bowl does not touch the water. Heat the chocolate and cream, stirring, until the chocolate melts.

4 Remove the pear halves from the syrup and drain on paper towels. Place a pear half, rounded side up, and a scoop of ice cream on each of 4 dessert plates. Top each with a little of the chocolate sauce and garnish with the mint leaves.

Step 2

Step 3

Step 4

Preparation: 25 minutes
Cooking: 12 minutes
Chilling: 2 hours
Per serving: 313 cal; 4 g pro;
15 g fat; 46 g carb.

TYPICALLY FRENCH

Pears Belle Hélène, the French dessert classic, was first served after the 1864 Paris premiere of Jacques Offenbach's operetta, *La Belle Hélène*. Since its debut, this exquisite treat has achieved worldwide popularity.

COOKING TIP

You can easily make the chocolate sauce in the microwave oven. Place the cream and chocolate in a microwave-safe dish and heat at full power, stirring every 30 seconds, until melted and smooth.

SERVING TIPS

Small crisp cookies go very well with this delicate dessert. You can also serve a brandy snifter of pear spirits, such as Pear William.

CHERRY CLAFOUTI

FRANCE

This classic dessert of rural France consists of fruit—often sweet cherries—coated with a pancakelike batter and baked until golden brown. It's always served warm from the oven.

INGREDIENTS
(Serves 4)

- 10 ounces sweet cherries
- 10 ounces sour cherries
- 3 large eggs
- 2 tablespoons confectioners' sugar
- pinch of salt
- 1 cup milk
- ¼ cup all-purpose flour

IN ADDITION
- butter for the mold
- confectioners' sugar for sprinkling

INGREDIENT TIP

This dessert can also be prepared with other slightly tart fruits. Apricots, berries, and plums all work well here.

1 Wash the cherries and put some with stems aside for a garnish. Remove the stems from the rest of the cherries and remove the pits with a cherry pitter.

2 Preheat the oven to 425°F. Thoroughly grease the inside of an 8-inch round or oval gratin or baking dish.

Step 1

3 Whisk the eggs with the confectioners' sugar and salt until foamy. Little by little, gently whisk in the milk and flour.

4 Lay the pitted cherries evenly in the bottom of the pan. Evenly spoon the batter over the top.

Step 3

5 Place the clafouti in the center of the oven and bake for about 35 minutes, until the top is lightly browned.

6 Remove the clafouti from the oven and let it cool slightly, then sprinkle lightly with confectioners' sugar. Garnish with the reserved cherries and serve warm.

Step 4

Preparation: 25 minutes
Baking: 35 minutes
Per serving: 230 cal; 9 g pro; 8 g fat; 33 g carb.

TYPICALLY LIMOUSIN

Limousin is a predominantly agricultural region in South Central France, where the rural cuisine is simple but rich in variety. One of Limousin's most famous dessert dishes is the sweet-tart cherry clafouti.

COOKING TIPS

• When cherries are not in season, jarred ones can be used. Drain all the liquid and reduce the amount of confectioners' sugar to 1 teaspoon.

• The flour and milk must be very gently folded into the batter so it doesn't become heavy and wet.

SERVING TIP

Serve a vanilla sauce with this dish. Bring 1½ cups milk, 4 tablespoons sugar, 1 tablespoon cornstarch, and a split vanilla bean to a boil, whisking. Whisk in a beaten egg yolk and cook, stirring, for 2 minutes.

$\mathscr{I}$NDIVIDUAL LEMON SOUFFLÉS

FRANCE

These light and fluffy soufflés, flavored with aromatic lemon, are among the classic delicacies of French cuisine. You can make them quickly and easily at home.

INGREDIENTS
(Serves 4-6)

- 2 lemons
- 1 cup milk
- ¼ cup all-purpose flour
- ⅔ cup sugar
- 1 tablespoon butter
- 4 large eggs

IN ADDITION
- butter for the molds
- sugar for the molds
- confectioners' sugar for decoration

INGREDIENT TIP

If you wish, use another citrus fruit—such as orange or lime—instead of lemon. Just be sure to use a fruit that's not too sweet, or the slightly sour character of the soufflé will be lost.

1 Grease the inside bottoms of four 6-ounce serving molds and sprinkle with sugar. Preheat the oven to 375°F. Wash and dry the lemons. Use a vegetable peeler to peel off the yellow peel. With a small sharp knife, cut the peel into thin strips. Halve the lemons and squeeze out the juice.

2 In a medium saucepan, whisk together 6 tablespoons of the milk and the flour. Gradually whisk in the remaining milk. Add ⅓ cup of the sugar and the butter and cook over low heat, whisking constantly, until thick, about 5 minutes; remove from heat.

3 Separate the eggs. Whisk together the yolks, lemon juice, and lemon peel. Whisk 2 tablespoons of the batter into the yolk mixture, then add the yolks to the pan with the batter and whisk well.

4 Beat the egg whites with the remaining ⅓ cup sugar until stiff; gently fold into the batter. Divide batter among the molds.

5 Place the molds on a baking sheet on the lowest oven rack; bake for about 15 minutes, until golden. Sprinkle with confectioners' sugar and serve immediately.

Step 1

Step 2

Step 4

Preparation: 45 minutes
Baking: 15 minutes
Per serving: 333 cal; 9 g pro; 12 g fat; 48 g carb.

TYPICALLY FRENCH
The French place great value on the culinary arts. Sweet and savory soufflés, enjoyed at restaurants and bistros all over the country, are some of their most delicate creations.

COOKING TIP

The beaten egg whites in any soufflé are what cause its impressive rise and cloudlike texture. To ensure the lightest, fluffiest soufflé, make sure to beat the whites until they are stiff but not dry, and then gently and slowly fold them into the batter, taking care not to deflate them as you go.

SERVING TIP

A creamy dessert sauce is the traditional accompaniment to sweet soufflés. Try a tangerine sauce, a white chocolate sauce, or a custard sauce with this citrusy confection.

FRUIT COMPOTES—THREE WAYS

Try these sublime combinations of fruits—kiwi, berries, and a luscious tropical mix—in their own juices.

HONEY-TOPPED KIWI TREAT

Preparation: 15 minutes   Cooking: 5 minutes

NEW ZEALAND

(SERVES 4)
- 3 kiwis
- 2 apples
- 1 cup plus 3 tablespoons apple juice
- 3 tablespoons lemon juice
- 2 tablespoons sugar
- 1 cinnamon stick
- 10 ounces gooseberries
- 1 tablespoon cornstarch

FOR THE SAUCE
- 1 cup heavy cream
- 2 tablespoons honey
- ½ teaspoon vanilla extract

1 Peel the kiwis; cut into ¾-inch dice. Peel and core the apples; cut into ¾-inch dice.

2 In a large saucepan, combine 1 cup apple juice, the lemon juice, sugar, and cinnamon stick and bring to a boil over medium-high heat. Add the apples and gooseberries and cook for 2 minutes.

3 In a cup, mix the cornstarch with the remaining 3 tablespoons apple juice. Stir into the fruit mixture and boil until slightly thickened. Remove the cinnamon stick. Stir in the kiwis, cover, and refrigerate until cold.

4 In a small bowl, mix the cream, honey, and vanilla. Serve the sauce with the fruit.

MIXED BERRIES

Preparation: 15 minutes

GERMANY

(SERVES 4)
- 1 cup strawberries
- 1 cup cranberry juice cocktail
- 12 ounces currants or cranberries
- ⅓ cup dried sour cherries
- 2 tablespoons sugar
- 1 cinnamon stick
- ⅓ cup raspberries

FOR THE SAUCE
- 1 package (2¼ ounces) vanilla instant pudding mix
- 3 cups milk

SWEET 'N TANGY TROPICAL FRUIT

Preparation: 25 minutes   Cooking: 10 minutes

CARIBBEAN

(SERVES 4)
- ½ pineapple
- 1 mango
- 1 kiwi
- 1 banana
- 2 tablespoons lemon juice
- 1 cup plus 3 tablespoons orange juice
- 2 tablespoons sugar
- 2 tablespoons white rum
- 1 cinnamon stick
- 1 tablespoon cornstarch
- 3 tablespoons toasted shredded coconut

2 In a large saucepan, mix the lemon juice, 1 cup orange juice, the sugar, rum, and cinnamon stick and bring to a boil. Add the pineapple and mango and cook for 6 minutes. Mix the cornstarch with the remaining 3 table-spoons orange juice and stir into the fruit. Boil for 2 minutes, until slightly thickened. Add the kiwi and banana and gently mix. Cover and refrigerate until cold.

3 Remove the cinnamon stick from the fruit mixture. Sprinkle the coconut on top.

1 Trim, peel, and core the pineapple. Peel the mango and cut the flesh from the pit. Peel the kiwi and banana. Cut the fruit into 1-inch pieces.

AND VANILLA SAUCE

Cooking: 12 minutes

1 Hull the strawberries and set aside. Combine the cranberry juice cocktail, currants, cherries, sugar, and cinnamon stick in a medium saucepan and bring to a boil. Cook for 2 minutes.

2 Stir the raspberries and strawberries into the cranberry mixture. Cover and refrigerate until cold.

3 Make the pudding with the milk according to the directions on the package. Remove the cinnamon stick from the fruit. Serve the sauce with the fruit.

SERVING TIP This Mediterranean dessert favorite is best when it's followed by a cup of real Italian espresso—the delicious strong, dark coffee traditionally served in tiny cups.

ZABAGLIONE WITH RED BERRIES

ITALY

Zabaglione, the delectably fluffy, wine-laced custard from the volcanic island of Sicily, is a wonderfully simple dessert. Here, it's a creamy bed for bright fresh berries.

INGREDIENTS
(Serves 4)

- 1 small lemon
- 2 cups assorted red berries (raspberries, strawberries, red currants)
- 5 tablespoons sugar
- 4 egg yolks
- ¼ cup Marsala wine
- mint leaves for garnish

INGREDIENT TIPS

- Local fresh-picked berries are especially good, so it's worthwhile shopping around for them.
- Marsala is a Sicilian wine that ranges from very sweet to dry—choose a sweet variety for this recipe. If you can't find it, use another fortified wine, such as sherry or port, instead.

1 With a fine grater, remove the lemon peel onto a sheet of waxed paper and set aside. Squeeze the juice into a large bowl.

2 Place the raspberries in the bowl with the lemon juice. Hull the strawberries. Cut in half or quarter if large and leave the small ones whole. Add to the raspberries. Strip off the stems of the currants with a fork and add them to the other berries. Sprinkle the berries with 1 tablespoon sugar and toss gently. Cover and refrigerate for 1 hour.

3 Whisk together the remaining ¼ cup sugar, the egg yolks, and the grated lemon peel in a large heatproof bowl. Place the bowl over simmering water. Whisk in the Marsala a tablespoon at a time, until the mixture is foamy and doubled in volume, about 5 minutes. Remove the bowl from the pan and whisk until cool.

4 Divide the zabaglione among 4 large stemmed glasses, add the berries, and garnish with the mint leaves. Serve at once, while the custard is still fluffy.

Step 1

Step 2

Step 3

Preparation: 15 minutes
Chilling: 1 hour
Cooking: 3 minutes
Per serving: 174 cal; 3 g pro;
5 g fat; 25 g carb.

TYPICALLY SICILIAN

Sweets are much loved on the isle of Sicily, where they play a role in virtually every holiday and celebration. In the words of one Sicilian writer: "Every sweet represents a fact. Every dessert is an episode."

ℐTUFFED PEACHES

ITALY

Here's a summer delight from Piedmont—sweet, juicy peaches with a scrumptious cookie filling. Briefly baked in a casserole and served warm, this dessert is alluringly fragrant.

INGREDIENTS
(Serves 4)

- 8 natural almonds
- 4 large peaches
- 3 tablespoons butter
- 3 ounces Amaretti (almond cookies) or biscuit cookies
- ¼ cup dry Marsala (secco)
- 1 large egg yolk
- 2 tablespoons sugar
- 1 tablespoon lemon juice

IN ADDITION

- confectioners' sugar for sprinkling
- fresh mint leaves

INGREDIENT TIPS

• Amaretti are small Italian almond cookies. Almond biscotti can be substituted with equally delicious results.
• If you can't find Marsala, dry sherry makes a good substitute for it.

1 Preheat the oven to 400°F. Grease a casserole dish with 1 tablespoon butter. Blanch the almonds for 2–3 minutes in boiling water. Drain and let cool. Slip the skins off the nuts by pressing them between your fingers.

2 Blanch peaches briefly in boiling water. Drain and peel with a small knife. Halve the peaches and remove the pits. Partially hollow out the halves with a spoon. Mash the removed flesh (about 2 tablespoons per peach) in a bowl using a fork.

3 Crumble the Amaretti cookies into the mashed peach pulp. Stir in the Marsala, egg yolk, sugar, and lemon juice. Arrange the peach halves cut-side up in the casserole dish, then fill them with the amaretti mixture. Decorate each peach half with a peeled almond.

4 Dot the tops of the peaches with the remaining 2 tablespoons butter. Bake for about 15 minutes, until the tops are browned. Sprinkle with confectioners' sugar and garnish with mint leaves before serving.

Step 1

Step 2

Step 3

Preparation: 35 minutes
Baking: 15 minutes
Per serving: 316 cal; 4 g pro; 14 g fat; 44 g carb.

TYPICALLY PIEDMONT
The sweet tooth of the Piedmontese is well-known. Cafes and confectioners keep residents well-supplied with seasonal treats. The ever-popular *pesche ripiene* (stuffed peaches) originated here.

COOKING TIP

It's not absolutely necessary to peel the skins off the peaches—the choice is yours. If you decide to scald and peel them, don't leave the peaches in hot water too long, or they'll get soft and lose flavor. Nectarines, which don't have to be peeled, also work well here.

SERVING TIP

A glass of semidry or sweet Marsala goes very well with this dessert.

$\mathscr{K}$ITCHEN GLOSSARY

Here's a simple guide to cooking terms and ingredients, plus a few tips that will come in handy while you're making fruit desserts.

GREAT DESSERT FRUITS

Many of these come to us from distant warm-weather lands.

Avocado

The creamy pulp of this green, pear-shaped fruit tastes mild and slightly nutty. Avocados should never be cooked, since they'll lose their flavor.

Coconut

Within the hard shell is the firm, white coconut meat, and within that is the sweet-sour coconut water which is a

favorite beverage in many parts parts of the world. Use a corkscrew to open two of the three sprout pores and pour the coconut water into a container. To open the shell, knock it firmly around the middle with a hammer.

Figs

Middle Eastern and Mediterranean recipes have made these small fruits popular. When ripe, fresh figs are very soft and sweet—and packed with tiny edible seeds.

Guava

A small greenish, yellow, or red oval or round fruit that has a sweet aroma and an intense flavor. Its meaty flesh may be packed with seeds or almost seedless.

Kiwi

Cultivated in California and New Zealand, this egg-shaped fruit has brown furry skin and a sweet, juicy, bright green interior. Skinned and sliced crosswise, kiwis make beautiful additions to fruit desserts.

Litchi

This small, sweet, rough-skinned fruit hails from China. Its translucent white flesh is often eaten plain or in fruit salads.

Mango

The bright yellow-orange flesh of the mango tastes something like an earthy peach. The ripe fruit, which gives slightly to the touch, is extremely fragrant, juicy, and flavorful.

Papaya

The orange flesh of the papaya is juicy and smooth and surrounds a cavity filled with shiny black seeds. Ripe papaya goes very well in fruit salads.

CARAMEL

A golden to brown confection that, depending on temperature, may be a syrupy liquid or a

brittle solid. It's made by simply melting sugar. (Soft caramel contains milk and butter as well.)

CITRUS FRUITS

Oranges, lemons, and their relatives are terrific flavor accents. For whole pieces, use a sharp knife to separate segments from their membranes. Use a vegetable peeler or zester to get long, thin strips of skin, called zest, without removing the bitter white pith. You

can also rub the skin of a citrus fruit with a sugar cube to extract aromatic oils. Simply add the sugar to the dish you are making.

COMPOTE
A chilled or warm dessert made of fresh or dried fruit, traditionally cooked in sugar syrup.

COCONUT MILK
A creamy liquid made from the white meat of coconuts. Simmer dried or freshly grated coconut meat and water until frothy, then strain through cheesecloth, squeezing to extract as much liquid as possible. Canned coconut milk is available at specialty-food markets.

CREAM OF TARTAR
A white powder that forms on the inside of wine barrels and is used to give a creamy consistency to sweets and frosting mixtures.

FLAMBÉ
French for "flamed" or "flaming," flambé is the beautiful effect produced by burning off alcohol that's poured over a dessert. Hard spirits—like whiskey, rum, or brandy— work best. Once it's lit, the alcohol evaporates while its flavors penetrate the food. Fruit is well suited to this technique.

GELATIN
Commonly available in packets of powder, gelatin expands when it's soaked in cool water, then gently heated. A popular ingredient in chilled fruit desserts, it becomes a clear jelly when cool.

MAPLE SYRUP
The pale to deep amber syrup of the sugar maple tree has a very sweet, light walnut aroma.

TRIFLE
A traditional English dessert consisting of sponge cake soaked in sherry or other spirits and layered with fruit and custard.

WHIPPED EGG WHITE
For firmer whipped egg whites, add a dash of salt, cream of tartar, or lemon juice before beating. Use room temperature eggs to get the best volume.

ZABAGLIONE
A luscious Italian custard that's made by whisking together egg yolks, sugar, and sweet wine. It can be served as a dessert in itself—often topped with berries or sliced fruit—or as a sauce over cakes, ice creams, or pastries.

SPICES AND FLAVORINGS
These ingredients give many desserts their unique allure.

Anise
The seeds of this plant have long been used to add a hint of licoricelike flavor to both sweet and savory foods.

Rose water
A rose-petal extract used to flavor sweets, especially those from the Middle East and India. It's available in drugstores and specialty markets.

Vanilla
Genuine vanilla is available in bean or extract form. To remove the flavorful seeds from the bean, split it lengthwise with a small sharp knife. Scrape out the seeds with the knife tip.

Cinnamon
The dried bark of the cinnamon tree tastes slightly sweet and is a popular spice for cakes and desserts. It is available ground or in sticks.

MENU SUGGESTIONS

For each of our light desserts, we present an appetizer and a main course. Look no further when you need ideas for entertaining your friends or family.

JAMAICA

MANGO AND COCONUT MOUSSE P. 6
*Lime-Grilled Shrimp
Rum and Honey–
Glazed Chicken*

—✦—

BARBADOS

TROPICAL FRUIT SALAD WITH RUM SAUCE P. 8
*Tomato and Orange Soup
Creole Steak
with Beans and Rice*

—✦—

THE BAHAMAS

CARIBBEAN ORANGE BASKETS P. 10
*Tomato and
Crabmeat Salad
Coconut Fried Chicken*

—✦—

MEXICO

TEQUILA-SPLASHED PINEAPPLE AND BANANA P. 12
*Guacamole
Chicken Enchiladas*

—✦—

USA

PEACH-BLUEBERRY COBBLER P. 14
*Salad Greens with Bacon
Grilled Pork Chops with Peas
and New Potatoes*

—✦—

BOURBON-BANANA FLAMBÉ P. 16
*Fried Zucchini
Grilled Tuna Steaks*

—✦—

CANADA

SWEET MAPLE FRUIT DELIGHT P. 18
*Smoked Salmon Canapés
Chicken Fricassee*

—✦—

NEW ZEALAND

LUSCIOUS KIWI-STRAWBERRY SALAD P. 20
*Rosemary Potatoes
Roast Leg of Lamb*

—✦—

THAILAND

CREAMY COCONUT RICE WITH FRUIT P. 24
*Coconut Chicken Soup
Spicy Barbecued Beef*

—✦—

CHINA

CHINESE TOFFEE APPLES P. 26
*Vegetable Stir-fry
Sweet-and-Sour Pork*

—✦—

ISRAEL

TANGY ORANGE-AVOCADO SALAD P. 28
*Eggplant Dip
with Pita
Marinated Beef Kabobs*

—✦—

IRAN

ORANGE ICE DREAM P. 30
*Cucumbers with Yogurt
Beef with Rice and
Chickpeas*

— ✦ —

SCOTLAND

**RASPBERRY CREAM
PARFAITS** P. 32
*Cock-a-leekie Soup
Steak with Pepper Sauce*

— ✦ —

ENGLAND

**TRADITIONAL ENGLISH
TRIFLE** P. 34
*Broiled Tomatoes
Roast Beef*

— ✦ —

DENMARK

**SPARKLING FRUIT
GELATIN RING** P. 36
*Creamy Sorrel Soup
Baked Halibut*

— ✦ —

UKRAINE

TIPSY STRAWBERRIES P. 38
*Mushroom and Potato Gratin
Roasted Chicken Breast*

— ✦ —

GERMANY

PLUM-APRICOT COMPOTE
P. 40
*Potato Soup
Classic Sauerbraten*

— ✦ —

SUMMER FRUIT SALAD P. 42
*Celery Salad with
Roasted Hazelnuts
Pan-Roasted Trout*

— ✦ —

AUSTRIA

**CINNAMON-APPLE
FRITTERS** P. 44
*Sautéed Cabbage
with Caraway
Veal Stew and
Potato Dumplings*

— ✦ —

SWITZERLAND

CHERRY BEIGNETS P. 46
*Onion Pie
Sliced Steak with
French-Fried Potatoes*

— ✦ —

FRANCE

PEARS BELLE HÉLÈNE
P. 48
*Mushrooms with Mustard
and Brandy
Beef Bourguignonne*

— ✦ —

CHERRY CLAFOUTI P. 50
*Onion Soup
Roast Duck with
Chestnuts*

— ✦ —

**INDIVIDUAL LEMON
SOUFFLÉS** P. 52
*Asparagus Vinaigrette
Veal Chops with Morels*

— ✦ —

ITALY

**ZABAGLIONE WITH
RED BERRIES** P. 56
*Marinated Peppers
Tuscan Chicken and
Parmesan Roast Potatoes*

— ✦ —

STUFFED PEACHES P. 58
*Bruschetta with Garlic
and Mozzarella
Linguini Puttanesca*

— ✦ —

63

$\mathcal{R}$ECIPE INDEX

Photo Credits
Book cover and recipe photos:
©International Masters Publishers AB
Michael Brauner, Dorothee Gödert, Neil Mersh
Agency photographs:
Introduction: Bavaria: Reinhard, page 5 upper right. Calorific: Moore/Blackstar, page 4 center left.
Cephas: Webb, page 4 lower left. Image Bank: Romanelli, page 5 center right.
Schapowalow: Heaton, page 4 upper left. Silvestris: Wagner, pages 4, 5 center.
Photos for the "Typically" sections:
Bavaria: Benelux Press, page 9; PP, page 16; Picture Finders, page 37; Wisniewski, page 40;
Reinhard, page 44; Higuchi, page 47.
Bilder Pur: Uselmann, page 42. IFA: Romann, page 10.
Image Bank: Castaneda, page 6; Curto, page 20.
Helga Lade: Bramaz, page 26; TPH, page 34; Siwak, page 38; Lowes, page 52; Pictures, page 57.
Schapowalow: Reichelt, page 24; Loos, pages 28, 31; Pratt-Press, pages 32, 50; Atlantide, page 58.
Silvestris: Pani/Jeske, page 12; Prato, page 14.
Tony Stone: Randly, page 19; Camille, page 48.